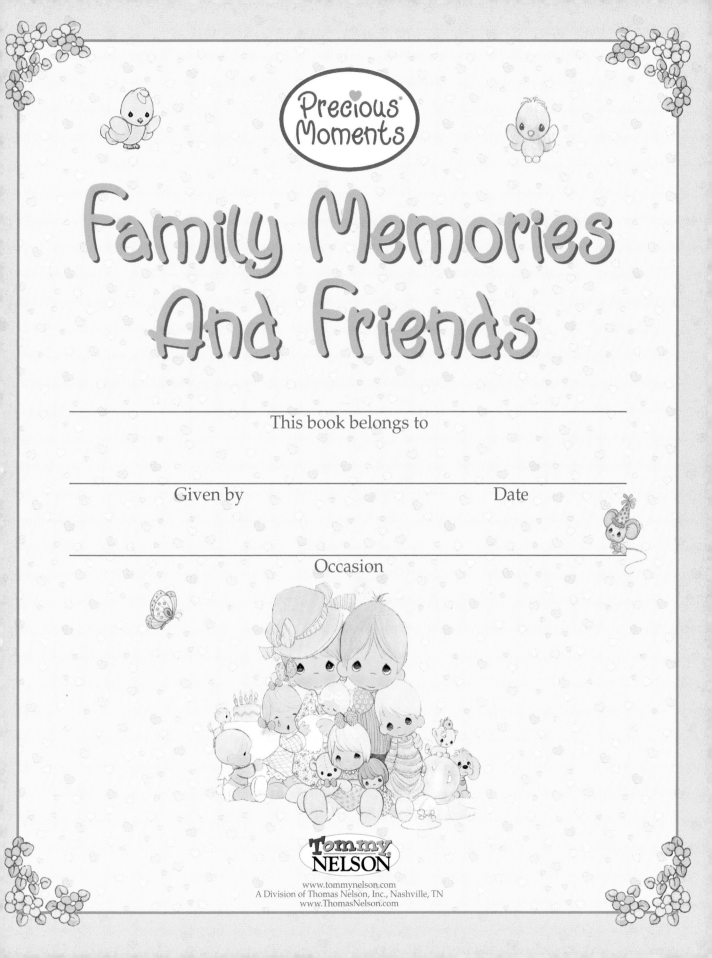

Precious Moments

Family Memories And Friends

_____

This book belongs to

_____

Given by   Date

_____

Occasion

Tommy NELSON

www.tommynelson.com
A Division of Thomas Nelson, Inc., Nashville, TN
www.ThomasNelson.com

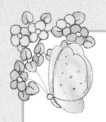

Introduction for Parents

Dear Parents,

What better way to share the special times of life with your children than with moments spent together reading the Bible? All through the year you and your children experience holidays, joyous events, fun times and even sad times. Wouldn't it be nice to highlight each celebration or event with a happy memory of learning God's word for that significant time? Wouldn't you also like to have them learn about the special characters in the Bible? So many of the well-known people in scripture are much like the friends your children meet every day. This colorful volume combines the fabric of family memories and friends!

Heritage is woven from family memories. We remember those special experiences. . . . Bible truth is learned with joy in the context of happy family memories we want to cherish forever. Included in this book are

special sections on Christmas, Easter, Thanksgiving, birthdays, and many more occasions to help make those family memories last forever in the hearts and minds of your little ones.

Also included in this volume is a section featuring some of the most well-known Bible characters. Each one combines verses from the International Children's Bible® translation along with the sweet and whimsical art of Sam Butcher's beloved Precious Moments® characters. The children playfully illustrate the scriptures and help tell the story about our favorite Bible friends. The titles also reflect the attribute of each story's character.

The last section includes a place for you and your child to record your own favorite family memories and friends. It is our sincere hope that this adorable book will become a cherished family heirloom, reminding you and your children of times spent reading the Bible and reminiscing over special family memories.

The Publisher

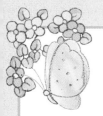

Table of Contents

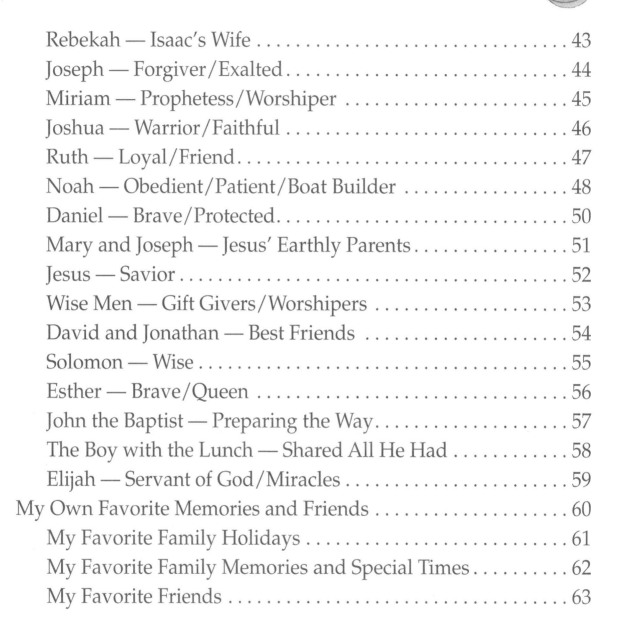

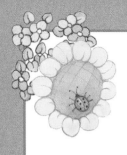

Christmas

Come, let's bow down and worship him.

Let's kneel before the Lord who made us. (Psalm 95:6)

"She will give birth to a son. You will name the son Jesus. Give him that name because he will save his people from their sins." (Matthew 1:21)

The angel came to her and said, "Greetings! The Lord has blessed you and is with you. . . . Don't be afraid, Mary, because God is pleased with you. Listen! You will become pregnant. You will give birth to a son, and you will name him Jesus. He will be great, and the people will call him the

Son of the Most High. The Lord God will give him the throne of King David, his ancestor." (Luke 1:28, 30–32)

At that time, Augustus Caesar sent an order to all people in the countries that

were under Roman rule. The order said that they must list their names in a register. This was the first registration taken while Quirinius was governor of Syria. And everyone went to their own towns to be registered.

So Joseph left Nazareth, a town in Galilee. He went to the town of Bethlehem in Judea. This town was known as the town of David. Joseph went there because he was from the family of David. Joseph registered with Mary because she was engaged to marry him. (Mary was now pregnant.) While Joseph and Mary were in Bethlehem, the time came for her to have the baby. She gave birth to her first son. There were no rooms left in the inn. So she wrapped the baby with cloths and laid him in a box where animals are fed.

That night, some shepherds were in the fields nearby

watching their sheep. An angel of the Lord stood before them. The glory of the Lord was shining around them, and suddenly they became very frightened. The angel said to them, "Don't be afraid, because I am bringing you some good news. It will be a joy to all the people. Today your Savior was born in David's town. He is Christ, the Lord. This is how you will know him: You will find a baby wrapped in cloths and lying in a feeding box."

Then a very large group of angels from heaven joined the first angel. All the angels were praising God, saying:

"Give glory to God in heaven,
and on earth let there be peace
to the people who please God."

Then the angels left the shepherds and went back to heaven. The shepherds said to each other, "Let us go to Bethlehem and see this thing that has happened. We will see this thing the Lord told us about."

So the shepherds went quickly and found Mary and Joseph. And the shepherds saw the baby lying in a feeding box. Then they told what the angels had said about this child. Everyone was amazed when they heard what the

shepherds said to them. Mary hid these things in her heart; she continued to think about them. Then the shepherds went back to their sheep, praising God and thanking him for everything that they had seen and heard. It was just as the angel had told them. (Luke 2:1–20)

"For God loved the world so much that he gave his only Son. God gave his Son so that whoever believes in him may not be lost, but have eternal life." (John 3:16)

Thanksgiving

Thank the Lord because he is good.

His love continues forever. (1 Chronicles 16:34)

Let's come to him with thanksgiving.

Let's sing songs to him. (Psalm 95:2)

Come into his city with songs of thanksgiving.

Come into his courtyards with songs of praise.

Thank him, and praise his name.

The Lord is good. His love continues forever.

His loyalty continues from now on. (Psalm 100:4–5)

Easter

He was wounded for the
wrong things we did.
He was crushed for the
evil things we did.
The punishment,
which made us
well, was given
to him.
And we are healed
because of his
wounds.
(Isaiah 53:5)

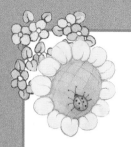

The angel said to the women, "Don't be afraid. I know that you are looking for Jesus, the one who was killed on the cross. But he is not here. He has risen from death as he said he would. Come and see the place where his body was." (Matthew 28:5–6)

"If anyone wants to follow me, he must say 'no' to the things he wants. Every day he must be willing even to die on a cross, and he must follow me." (Luke 9:23)

John said, "Look, the Lamb of God. He takes away the sins of the world!" (John 1:29)

Birthdays

This is the day that the Lord has made.

Let us rejoice and be glad today! (Psalm 118:24)

Every good action and every perfect gift is from God.

These good gifts come down from the Creator of the sun,

moon, and stars. (James 1:17)

Each of you received a spiritual gift. God has shown you his grace in giving you different gifts. And you are like servants who are responsible for using God's gifts. So be good servants and use your gifts to serve each other. (1 Peter 4:10)

New Baby

"May the Lord bless you and keep you.

May the Lord show you his kindness.

May he have mercy on you.

May the Lord watch over you and give you peace."

(Numbers 6:24–26)

Children are a gift from the Lord.

Babies are a reward. (Psalm 127:3)

"Before I made you in your mother's womb, I chose you. Before you were born, I set you apart for a special work." (Jeremiah 1:5)

Jesus said, "Let the little children come to me. Don't stop them, because the kingdom of heaven belongs to people who are like these children." (Matthew 19:14)

Passing on Memories and Traditions

Remember my words in your hearts and souls. Write them down and tie them to your hands as a sign. Tie them on your foreheads to remind you. Teach them well to your children. Talk about them when you sit at home and walk along the road. Talk about them when you lie down and when you get up. Write them on your doors and gates. Then both you and your children will live a long time in the land. This is the land the Lord promised your ancestors. You will live there for as long as the skies are above the earth. (Deuteronomy 11:18–21)

My son, keep your father's commands.

Don't forget your mother's teaching.

Remember their words forever.

Let it be as if they were tied around your neck.

They will guide you when you walk.

They will guard you while you sleep.

They will speak to you when you are awake.

(Proverbs 6:20–22)

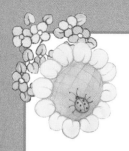

Train a child how to live the right way.

Then even when he is old, he will still live that way.

(Proverbs 22:6)

It always gives me the greatest joy when I hear that my children are following the way of truth. (3 John 4)

Vacations and Times of Recreation and Togetherness

He has put his angels in charge of you.

They will watch over you wherever you go. (Psalm 91:11)

There is a right time for everything.

Everything on earth has its special season. (Ecclesiastes 3:1)

Two people are better than one.

They get more done by working together.

If one person falls,

the other can help him up.

But it is bad for the person who is alone when he falls.

(Ecclesiastes 4:9–10)

If God wants me to, I will come to you. I will come with joy, and together you and I will have a time of rest. (Romans 15:32)

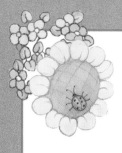

Laughter

I will rejoice in the Lord.

I will be happy when he saves me. (Psalm 35:9)

We were filled with laughter,

and we sang happy songs.

Then the other nations said,

"The Lord has done great things for them."

The Lord has done great things for us,

and we are very glad. (Psalm 126:2–3)

The Lord makes me very happy.

All that I am rejoices in my God. (Isaiah 61:10)

Love for Family

"Honor your father and your mother. Then you will live a long time in the land. The Lord your God is going to give you this land."

(Exodus 20:12)

Grandchildren are the reward of old people. And children are proud of their parents.

(Proverbs 17:6)

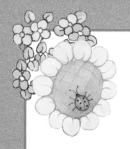

Love each other like brothers and sisters. Give your brothers and sisters more honor than you want for yourselves. (Romans 12:10)

Let us try to do what makes peace and helps one another. (Romans 14:19)

Do everything in love. (1 Corinthians 16:14)

Spiritual Memories

I will praise the Lord at all times.

His praise is always on my lips. (Psalm 34:1)

Shout to the Lord, all the earth.

Serve the Lord with joy.

Come before him with singing. (Psalm 100:1–2)

I was happy when they said to me,

"Let's go to the Temple of the Lord." (Psalm 122:1)

God is in the light. We should live in the light, too. If we live in the light, we share fellowship with each other. And when we live in the light, the blood of the death of Jesus, God's Son, is making us clean from every sin. (1 John 1:7)

Loss of a Friend or Loved One

The Lord is my shepherd.

I have everything I need.

He gives me rest in green pastures.

He leads me to calm water.

He gives me new strength.

For the good of his name,

he leads me on paths that are right.

Even if I walk

through a very dark valley,

I will not be afraid

because you are with me.

Your rod and your walking stick comfort me.

(Psalm 23:1–4)

favorite family friends

Moses

Leader

The Lord answered, "I myself will go with you. And I will give you victory."

Then Moses said to him, "If you yourself don't go with us, then don't send us away from this place. If you don't go with us, no one will know that you are pleased with me and your people. These people and I would be no different from any other people on earth."

Then the Lord said to Moses, "I will do what you ask. This is because I know you very well, and I am pleased with you."
(Exodus 33:14–17)

Isaac

Promised One/Sacrifice

Sarah said, "God has made me laugh. Everyone who hears about this will laugh with me. No one thought that I would be able to have Abraham's child. But I have given Abraham a son while he is old." (Genesis 21:6–7)

The angel said, "Don't kill your son or hurt him in any way. Now I can see that you respect God. I see that you have not kept your son, your only son, from me." (Genesis 22:12)

Rebekah

Isaac's Wife

Laban and Bethuel answered, "This is clearly from the Lord. We cannot change what must happen. Rebekah is yours. Take her and go. Let her marry your master's son as the Lord has commanded." (Genesis 24:50–51)

Then Isaac brought Rebekah into the tent of Sarah, his mother. And she became his wife. Isaac loved her very much. So he was comforted after his mother's death. (Genesis 24:67)

Joseph

Forgiver/Exalted

Joseph said to them, "Come close to me." So the brothers came close to him. And he said to them, "I am your brother Joseph. You sold me as a slave to go to Egypt. Now don't be worried. Don't be angry with yourselves because you sold me here. God sent me here ahead of you to save people's lives. . . . So it was not you who sent me here, but God. God has made me the highest officer of the king of Egypt. I am in charge of his palace. I am the master of all the land of Egypt. (Genesis 45:4–5, 8)

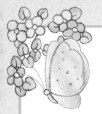

Miriam

Prophetess/Worshiper

Aaron's sister Miriam, who was a prophetess, took a tambourine in her hand. All the women followed her, playing tambourines and dancing. Miriam told them:

> "Sing to the Lord
> because he is worthy of great honor."
> (Exodus 15:20–21)

Joshua
Warrior/Faithful

Joshua son of Nun was then filled with wisdom. Moses had put his hands on Joshua. So the Israelites listened to Joshua. And they did what the Lord had commanded Moses. (Deuteronomy 34:9)

On the seventh day they got up at dawn. They marched around the city seven times. They marched just as they had on the days before. But on that day they marched around the city seven times. The seventh time around the priests blew their trumpets. Then Joshua gave the command: "Now, shout! The Lord has given you this city!" . . . When the priests blew the trumpets, the people shouted. At the sound of the trumpets and the people's shout, the walls fell. And everyone ran straight into the city. So the Israelites defeated that city. (Joshua 6:15–16, 20)

Ruth

Loyal/friend

Ruth said, "Don't ask me to leave you! Don't beg me not to follow you! Every place you go, I will go. Every place you live, I will live. Your people will be my people. Your God will be my God. And where you die, I will die. And there I will be buried. I ask the Lord to punish me terribly if I do not keep this promise: Only death will separate us." (Ruth 1:16–17)

Noah

Obedient/Patient/Boat Builder

God said to Noah and his sons . . . "I make this agreement with you: I will never again destroy all living things by floodwaters. A flood will never again destroy the earth. . . . I am putting my rainbow in the clouds. It is the sign of the agreement between me and the earth. When I bring clouds over the earth, a rainbow appears in the clouds. Then I will remember my agreement. It is between me and you and every living thing. Floodwaters will never again destroy all life on the earth. (Genesis 9:8, 11, 13–15)

Daniel

Brave/Protected

As he came near the den, he was worried. He called out to Daniel. He said, "Daniel, servant of the living God! Has your God that you always worship been able to save you from the lions?"

Daniel answered, "My king, live forever! My God sent his angel to close the lions' mouths. They have not hurt me, because my God knows I am innocent. I never did anything wrong to you, my king." (Daniel 6:20–22)

Mary and Joseph

Jesus' Earthly Parents

During Elizabeth's sixth month of pregnancy, God sent the angel Gabriel to a virgin who lived in Nazareth, a town in Galilee. She was engaged to marry a man named Joseph from the family of David. Her name was Mary. . . . The angel said to her, "Don't be afraid, Mary, because God is pleased with you. Listen! You will become pregnant. You will give birth to a son, and you will name him Jesus. He will be great, and people will call him the Son of the Most High. The Lord God will give him the throne of King David, his ancestor. He will rule over the people of Jacob forever. His kingdom will never end." (Luke 1:26–27, 30–33)

Jesus

Savior

The angel said to the women, "Don't be afraid. I know that you are looking for Jesus, the one who was killed on the cross. But he is not here. He has risen from death as he said he would. Come and see the place where his body was." (Matthew 28:5–6)

The Word became a man and lived among us. We saw his glory—the glory that belongs to the only Son of the Father. The Word was full of grace and truth. (John 1:14)

Wise Men

Gift Givers/Worshipers

They asked, "Where is the baby who was born to be the king of the Jews? We saw his star in the east. We came to worship him." (Matthew 2:2)

David and Jonathan

Best Friends

Jonathan said to David, "Go in peace. We have promised by the Lord that we will be friends. We said, 'The Lord will be a witness between you and me, and between our descendants forever.'" Then David left, and Jonathan went back to town. (1 Samuel 20:42)

RiP!

Solomon

Wise

While he was at Gibeon, the Lord came to him in a dream during the night. God said, "Ask for anything you want. I will give it to you." Solomon answered . . . "Lord my God, you have allowed me to be king in my father's place. But I am like a little child. I do not have the wisdom to do what I must do. . . . So I ask that you give me wisdom. Then I can rule the people in the right way. Then I will know the difference between right and wrong. Without wisdom, it is impossible to rule this great people of yours."

(1 Kings 3:5–7, 9)

Esther

Brave/Queen

Mordecai gave orders to say to Esther: "Just because you live in the king's palace, don't think that out of all the Jews you alone will escape. You might keep quiet at this time. Then someone else will help and save the Jews. But you and your father's family will all die. And who knows, you may have been chosen queen for just such a time as this."

Then Esther sent this answer to Mordecai: "Go and get all the Jews in Susa together. For my sake, give up eating. Do not eat or drink for three days, night and day. I and my servant girls will also give up eating. Then I will go to the king, even though it is against the law. And if I die, I die." (Esther 4:13–16)

John the Baptist

Preparing the Way

John was baptizing people in the desert. He preached a baptism of changed hearts and lives for the forgiveness of sins. . . . This is what John preached to the people: "There is one coming later who is greater than I. I am not good enough even to kneel down and untie his sandals. I baptize you with water. But the one who is coming will baptize you with the Holy Spirit." (Mark 1:4, 7–8)

The Boy
with the Lunch

Shared All He Had

Andrew said, "Here is a boy with five loaves of barley bread and two little fish. But that is not enough for so many people."

Then Jesus took the loaves of bread. He thanked God for the bread and gave it to the people who were sitting there. He did the same with the fish. He gave them as much as they wanted.

They all had enough to eat. When they had finished, Jesus said to his followers, "Gather the pieces of fish and bread that were not eaten. Don't waste anything." So they gathered up the pieces that were left. They filled 12 large baskets with the pieces that were left of the five barley loaves. (John 6:9, 11–13)

Elijah

Servant of God/Miracles

Elijah said to her, "Don't worry. Go home and cook your food as you have said. But first make a small loaf of bread from the flour you have. Bring it to me. Then cook something for yourself and your son. The Lord, the God of Israel, says, 'That jar of flour will never become empty. The jug will always have oil in it. This will continue until the day the Lord sends rain to the land.'" . . . The jar of flour and the jug of oil were never empty. This happened just as the Lord, through Elijah, said it would. (1 Kings 17:13–14, 16)

My Own
favorite
Memories
and friends

My favorite
Family Holidays

_____

_____

_____

_____

_____

_____

_____

_____

_____

_____

My Favorite Family Memories and Special Times

Church _____

_____

_____

_____

_____

Vacations _____

_____

_____

_____

_____

My favorite friends

_____

_____

_____

_____

_____

Dear God, thank you for loving me.
Thank you for this day
and the beautiful world I live in.
Thank you for family and friends
to play and share with.
Thank you for my home —
for clothes and food
and a safe place to be.
Thank you for my church
and for those who are teaching me.
Dear God, help me to do
what you want me to do.
Forgive me when I do wrong things —
when I hurt myself and those around me.
Forgive me when I hurt you.
Make me want to be the very best
that I can be.
Amen.